Songs Unspoken
(VOL.2)

OTHER BOOKS BY FRANK ALEXANDER WRAY

SONGS UNSPOKEN (vol.1)

SHADOW DAWN

THE CIVIL WAR
The Journal of Martha Wayles Robertson

WHEN CLOWNS CRY

SWEET SOUTHERN DAYS

Songs Unspoken

(VOL.2)

Frank Alexander Wray

 www.trafford.com

North America & International
toll-free: 1 888 232 4444 (USA & Canada)
phone: 250 383 6864 ♦ fax: 812 355 4082

CONTENTS

TO:

THOSE WHO CANNOT SPEAK FOR THEMSELVES

"Imagination is greater than knowledge..." Einstein

ABOUT THE AUTHOR

Frank Alexander Wray used to reside on the historical Eastern Shore of Virginia, a narrow peninsula surround by the Chesapeake Bay and the Atlantic Ocean. It is here that he first started to become interested in the craft of writing at a very young age. Today, he writes poetry, children's stories, and non-fiction and fiction.

He was educated at Broadwater Academy, Exmore, Virginia, the Eastern Shore Community College, Melfa, Virginia, and Virginia Tech, Blacksburg, Virginia. Although he was very successful at the time in his chosen field of mechanical contracting, his paramount interest in life has always been writing. His efforts in writing since a child have always been focused toward humanitarian conditions.

Today he resides in Saint Augustine, Florida.

ABOUT THE BOOK

SONGS UNSPOKEN, Volume I, ISBN: 0-533-10030-5, was published in 1992. The book is now out of print and due to requests, I decided to write Volume II. I have made three additions of a series of verse giving testimony to the children being abused, the wrongfully committed, and the innocent in our penal system. These selections of poetry are moving, as each of the poems shows the reader the awful consequences of confinement. In each series of verse, a time of healing is offered so the victim can find a peace and trust and be able to move on in a positive direction. The poetry of Volume I, The Homeless, is also included in this selection of verse.

This universal read is needed for today's turbulent world, and is intended for all readers in all walks of life. It has been my intention to write for humanitarian conditions, and I will keep that promise to the reader and myself. There are times when "Life gets in the way," as I have always said. Now, those innocent souls who have lost a place in the world have someone to speak for them in a time of despair.

A SPECIAL THANKS TO:

Those with no shelter, those suffering with abuse, those innocently committed to state mental hospitals against their will, those wrongly accused and serving sentences in the penal system. These are people who are the real heroes of the world. Without them, this book of verse could not have been written to help others facing the same trauma. Without them, there would be no story to tell for humanity.

…Frank Alexander Wray

FOREWORD

When I think of Frank, who I have known for over 40 years, the first word that comes to mind is fighter. For most, that word brings up athletic images and Frank was certainly a competitor starting in our early days of youth baseball on opposing teams. Later, in high school, he reveled in the intensity and teamwork of football inspired by a coach he loved. But more than that, to me the word fighter describes an individual who has faced and overcome adversity well beyond what most people will experience. He has maintained humility and yet gained an empathy gleaned from physical and emotional pain. He has lived many years with debilitating diseases, misdiagnoses, hospitalizations and multiple surgeries, all of which should have defeated him. He has baffled doctors with his ability to keep a positive outlook in spite of the negative odds. Out of his own pain, comes the empathy which has allowed him to find a written voice for those who do not have an audience or a venue to tell about their own plight. Being a fighter helps him keep his head up, laugh about good memories and feel for those whom he says have not been as fortunate as he. He is a good friend, a brother in Christ and a lesson on perseverance to those who know him well.

...Mike Lewendowski

INTRODUCTION

This book of verse, SONGS UNSPOKEN, Volume II, was written with one goal in mind and that was to give testimony to the innocent who are unable to speak for themselves. Within these pages are observations I have concluded about the homeless, the abused, those wrongfully committed to state mental hospitals, and those innocent serving sentences in the penal system. These words are, hopefully, to give comfort to those suffering with a heavy burden so they can someday return and be a productive part of society. This book was intended for humanity on a universal basis.

It was often told to me by my grandmother to "place a word in a phrase so it will grow, like a flower in a garden. If a word does not reach out in all directions, it will not expand and will want to be moved or it will die. It is the same way with a flower, as it will tell you if it likes its spot where you have planted it." I have always paid strict attention to those words of wisdom in my life. Words are powerful, and should be meaningful by touching other words to give a full effect so the reader can gain a picture of what is being written. Equally, flowers are powerful as they reach to the admirer by beauty and fragrance and they, too, give a long lasting sense of heavenly delight to the mind, body, and spirit.

This book is divided into four sections, the first being SONGS UNSPOKEN, Volume II, those with no shelter. In this group of poems, I have shown the reader the circumstances of one living on the street. It could be any street in any town or city. It could be in any country in the world. It could be a mother or father, a brother or sister, a child, or any loved one. I have included all of humanity in these selections of poems. Sadly, my observations have concluded many of these people are a forgotten part of society and have fallen on their luck and only ask for a hand to get back on their feet. But much of society tends to look the other way, until the same misfortune happens to them one day.

The second section is titled REFLECTIONS, The Abused. This section pertains to my observations of those that were abused and how they survived the trauma and coped with the abuse on a daily basis. It is my hope that this selection of poetry will help those individuals to overcome such pain and suffering. This inspirational section includes seventeen poems which were extremely difficult to write but the overall picture had to have clarity for healing and so I was able to convey the message of those who were abused to help others confront this life-going tragedy.

The third section is titled THE GATES OF HELL, those wrongfully committed to state mental hospitals. Sadly, this trauma continues in this country and in the rest of the world today, even with all the superior medical technology and training in the medical and law professions. This was supposed to have ended in the 1940's but it never did stop. I have written about those people who are wrongly committed to these institutions and surely have spoken for the innocent, as they are unable to speak for themselves as they are drugged with antipsychotic drugs.

The fourth and final section is titled THE INNOCENT, those innocent serving sentences in the penal system. Although this section only includes one poem, it is extremely powerful in its message. It is my hope and wish it will reach out to those innocent for crimes they did not commit and to their loved ones and to the legal system.

Writing these songs of verse has been a challenge but a rewarding experience because I know if they help just one person, then it is all worthwhile. I have been fortunate to write over a thousand poems, and they all pertain to humanity in some way. My poetry sings a song: a song uplifting, a song to be heard, a song of cries for help, a song of peace, a song of hope, a song of love, a song for all humanity. Within the following pages of this book of verse, it is my profound wish that you, the reader, can find a special place in your heart for the less fortunate, the child that cannot tell, the one with no mind, and the one whose cries are never heard.

...Frank Alexander Wray

SONGS UNSPOKEN

Volume II

Those With No Shelter

Homeless

They walk the streets of every city,
The lonely trails along the way,
They have no aim, no goal, no home,
Patiently, objectively they carefully roam!
Strength at times almost perfect,
And yet they stumble on,
Reasoning cautiously,
And going by reason thus,
On they go, from day to day;
When hope is well not spent,
Still watching for a human friend,
To help to the journey's end,
When clouds hang low and twilight comes,
And cars, buses, trains rush by,
And these lonely-hearted people,
Most homesick for their native land,
And yet they must endure the lonely trail,
And restlessness grows with the years,
No sense to dread for their fears,
For they weep and stumble along the lonely way.

A Street Child

Look into one's eyes,
The child on the street,
Feel the lonely cries,
This precious child, nowhere to sleep;
A world full, but empty,
No food, no shelter, no love,
No warmth is theirs,
Faces smitten, noses running,
Mouths drooped, clothes torn,
Mind, body, soul worn,
All looking, no one seeing
The precious child—on the street,
No help, no hope
From strangers they meet.

Man in a Box

A man lay in a box,
Having no home,
Just taking all of life's knocks,
On the streets all alone;
Some give a dime, some a quarter,
Some just pass him by,
Some wish to commit murder,
Some just want to cry
For the Man in the box,
'Cause he is needy, helpless,
Listless, no bliss,
No hope—just despair;
But God continues to provide
When man turns away,
For man looks, never observes,
Just passing him by,
Street man trying to survive,
No help on his side,
Fellow-man, just walking away,
Giving no encouragement, yesterday or today,
Not even a helping hand,
To the man in the box,
Homeless man—in a box.

State Park

In any state park
Homeless sit on a bench—crouched,
Reading a book, making an idle remark,
Just passing time, and no trouble,
Belongings on one side,
And a dog on the other,
No home, no pride, no esteem,
Wondering and wondering
And cursing the world
For either—no hope, no direction,
Man in a soiled sweater, torn trousers,
No destiny, nowhere to run,
Another day—sadness,
Silently weeping, waiting,
And waiting—and praying
For someone, anyone, just someone.

The Bag Lady

She pushes a cart, and totes a bag,
Snacks on crumbs of stale food,
Once radiant clothes now rags,
People pass and appear rude,
Laced shoes—turned, stumbling along,
Dirty hair, smitten face,
A cold plight, no sweet song,
To sing—and no one to listen,
Horns a blowing, people waving,
Police parading, no peace within,
Humble bag lady, soul a-weeping,
No family—no friend.

The Needy

The gently falling snow,
With irregular flakes—so pure—so white,
Has covered the earth over and over,
With a garment that is crystal bright.

The rich and well-to-do,
There is much pleasure for their sake,
Hear the jingling of the sleigh bells,
They seem so happy, not even an ache.

But with the sick and poor, alas,
No pleasure will you find,
They dread the falling of the snow,
As something most unkind.

Oh! Poverty, Oh! Poverty, how great thy sting,
Much suffering the snow will bring,
The poor, the poor, how sad their lot,
When needing everything and having nothing.

Oh! Homeless, the cold, bitter cold, no warmth is theirs,
No fire burning bright,
But all is dark, despair, and dread to them,
For no food, warmth, shelter is in sight.

Homeless Momma and Child

Go to sleep, my precious child,
While the calm zephyrs blowing,
From their home in the West,
Lull thy tired form to rest,
For angels guard thee tonight!
Till the soft morning light,
Once again shines in your blue eyes
When—my precious child
It is time to arise.
And another day—more street lies,
Now sleep, my child,
Peace be with you—for a while.

Soup Kitchen

Clatter of dishes—silverware,
Clamor of homeless,
Soup's on—songs sung,
Behind Central Avenue
Confused children—women—men.

Aroma of food, peace for a while,
Tears—a few smiles,
Searching and searching for words to say,
To thank the staff on a rainy day,
For homeless come and go,
And the staff knows they suffer so.

Street People

A cart they push
Or wagon they pull
Chrome, rusty, wobbly,
A few belongings—and an apple maybe,
Staring at the cold ground,
And never around,
At you or me.
Just walking, stumbling,
Passing time—observing,
Reminiscing, mumbling,
Questioning when life begun,
Just pushing or pulling their load,
As wheels squeak and clatter
On every street corner
Your daughter—
Son—sister or brother,
Or perhaps
Mother or father.

A Shelter

Dear children, caring women, humble men,
No self-esteem, no hope,
No permanent home, but shelter tonight,
No friends—no kin,
Cot after cot
Row after row,
Some sleeping—others tossing,
Children crying—mothers, a weeping,
Together a family,
But separate no being,
Some ashamed, others guilty,
Men give up all hoped for,
All are tired, some sick, all are needy,
And a few curl up,
On the dusty floor.
Tonight shelter—tomorrow—
Well, tomorrow!
Maybe an open door.

Weeping

Do you see the child—on the street?
The little one—with no home,
No shoes on her feet,
Nowhere to call her own.

Do you see people walking by?
The child—helpless, homeless,
Today alive—tomorrow she may die,
Sickly—and you pass her by—ignoring all this.

Do you see the child beg? Humbly,
For something to eat,
For life began once—for her—for you—for me,
For her I pray; for you I weep.

Destitution

Tears fall to the pavement,
Others' tears remain dry;
The soul now weak and helpless,
The mind once indestructible,
So fragile—now cracks,
No value, only stress.
The heart once tender,
Now broken more or less,
And approaching homeless,
Through the door—or not,
Once strong—now lifeless;
Crawling through the corridor,
Such distress—a lull.
One hiding behind a door,
Those with such hurt,
Feel it in their face,
Human suffering, and disgrace,
To be saved by God's grace.
Assuming everything, expecting nothing.
Scuffling of feet,
Sweet sound I sing,
To homeless I meet,
For their plight is cold,
And courage so true,
A faith so bold,
And some—you even knew,
One's soul so deep.
Some Vietnam Vets,
On every city street.

Homeless Sister

She walks and walks
From sun to sun
And nowhere safe to sleep
No need to hide or run.

Look at your sister
See her slouched
On the wooden bus bench
Yeah! In front of the fancy church.

A brown bag of clothes
Hand clutching a pink blanket,
Yeah! Our black sister,
Nowhere to lay her head.

Wake up, America!
Your day's a-dawning—your sister's ending,
Wake up, America!
This is your homeless sister.

Behind the Streets of L.A.

And they lay a homeless child
On the curb,
Hair blonde, skin frail,
So innocent, despondent, pale,
Blood a-flowing—shot and suffering,
Behind the streets of L.A.
And for no reason—none,
For the gangs of L.A.
Such pity—no compassion
For humanity.
And behind the streets of L.A.
A homeless mother screams,
A homeless father cries,
For their little girl,
A precious soul,
Once vibrant,
Now silently succumbs
To the gentle hand of death
Behind the streets of L.A.

A Thought

Do you condemn one for
Being homeless,
Or praise one for
Their accomplishments?
Do you belittle one for
Their failure,
Or encourage one for
Their efforts?
Do you prejudge one for
Their misfortune,
Or judge one for
Their courage?

Homeless Prayer

Wants and needs along life's way,
How they crowd us, day by day,
Slipping in, but rarely out,
Things we see and dream about,
Now and then, a bit of lace,
How it stares us in the face,
Dainty, creamy, soft stuff,
Something nice, but never enough,
Ermine white and soft like down,
On the neck of someone's gown.
Just a want in days gone by,
Still remembered with a sigh,
There are fragile links of gold,
With a pendant seen of gold,
There are memories sweeter yet,
Than the things we would forget,
Not just wanted things but needs,
Not like ermine, lace and beads,
Tree's a-flame and sunset gold,
Evening shadows on the mold,
Far beyond this human sphere,
Things we've longed for every year,
Things we've seemed to need so much,
Far beyond our reach and touch,
We will find forever more,
When we homeless
Face the open door!

REFLECTIONS

(The abused)

Reflections

As I hold my child on my knee,
I gaze into those sparkling blue eyes,
Only to see the reflections of me,
All those yesterdays – lonely, lonely cries,
All those horrible visions I can now see.

As I comfort my precious child,
I wonder and I wonder how I once felt,
To be so close yet so far,
To my abuser, who left me with a deep scar.

As I softly speak to my dear child,
I recall the familiar voice of my abuser.

Left with my mind to imagine bliss,
My dear child, I remember all this.

As I stare and weep in the presence of my child,
I can only vision the once innocence of me,
My childhood so full of despair,
My dear child you could never know the sorrow,
And you will never see, no child should ever see,
These reflections that stare at me.

The Abused Children

Oh! Dear sweet children – I know you hurt so,
Still, always remember to trust your dreams,
For your courage will make all come true,
And most importantly, always listen with your heart,
'Cause, dear children, I feel what you feel too,
Just as a gorgeous garden of flowers,
Always vision life's happiest hours,
Forget those horrible thorns and briars,
Yes, my dear children, I know you hurt so,
And in your hours of sorrow and despair,
Remember my borrowed words will touch your heart,
'Cause these words are song of songs for your comfort,
Merely placed in your heart, my children of abuse.

A Victim's Home

Dilapidated, untenanted, all alone,
Roof worn and mossy, windows gone,
Sills brave and strong, after many a gale,
Door on creaking hinges still ajar.

Close to the old house, a giant box elder,
With boughs like human, understanding arms,
Leans tenderly toward the worn old roof,
Every fiber quivering with conscious glory,
And picture worthy of an artist's brush!

In the distance a stream surrounded in musical cadence,
And hills mirrored in its waters,
An undertone of peace and triumph they flow,
Understandingly, an old house – a victim's house.

The Closet

The familiar cracking floor,
As we walk to the cubicle,
And now he opens the door,
My heart pounding, now a lull.

The musty odor completely surrounds,
So dark, so very dark, such loneliness,
Staring in my eyes, he frowns,
And now the cubicle filled with emptiness.

Looking above, the wooden rod,
Lay beneath me, my clothes, my doll,
My sweaty hands caress the brown rod,
My name, if only someone would call.

Now a minute is an hour,
Tenderly touching, tenderly touching, now quivering,
I feel nothing, for I am no coward,
That touch, now nothing, now nothing.

Falling to the cold floor,
I cuddle my clothes, my doll,
Looking up, that frown, the wooden door,
Now I hear my momma call.

A Lullaby

Momma! Will you sing me a lullaby?
Oh! Please momma, sing me a lullaby,
Hold me Momma,
Oh! Please hold me, Momma.

Why do you let him hurt me, Momma?
Why do you come in here and hide,
I love you – do you love me, Momma?
Why Momma, why do you hide?

Momma, please sing me a lullaby,
Oh! Momma, I hurt so inside,
Just a soft song so I won't cry.

Oh! Momma, all I wanted was a lullaby,
And now no one to sing me a song,
What did I do wrong?
Now my Momma won't sing me a little lullaby.

The Bedroom

Footsteps, bedroom clutter, trembling
Prolongs the agony
As if no one was around,
Oh! The lonely soul, such turmoil,
Everyone asleep but I see a frown,
Next to my bed, sweating, now a lull,
My flesh no longer pure,
For beneath the bone and tissue,
The innermost part of me,
The realm of soul to spirit,
My abuser blind – cannot see
Dear God! Comfort me.

Sisterly Love

My dear sister and I together
Patient, strong and true,
Loving, sharing and helping each other,
Through childhood life together
In patches of thorns and dark shadows,
The emotional maze of pain
What do the tender years to offer?
To only us a glad refrain,
And beyond the innocent suffering,
The sisterly praise of glad release.

My Susie-Doll

I love to think of my Susie-doll,
My dear friend of childhood years,
My dear Susie-doll we did survive,
We were always by each other's side,
In my eyes you always stood so tall,
And now, finally, you are sheltered with other dolls,
Beloved, and free from tears,
The traces of your waxen cheeks,
Of tears you used to shed,
Are there because you protected me,
Yes, even when all the rest had gone to bed.

For you, my dear orphan child,
No longer sad but gay,
May the remainder days be happy hours,
With sweet dolls who like to play!
To my dear Susie-doll and all the rest,
So happy with each other,
I send my greetings, and my love,
For you, and all your surviving Mothers.

Inside Me

Now look into my eyes,
Tell me what you see,
Can you feel all the lonely cries,
Do you really see me.

Now look above my brow,
Tell me what you see,
Can you see the deep scars now,
Now could you have walked with me.

Now let us open this scar, tell me how you feel,
Can you take a glimpse afar,
Yes, it is all very real.

Now reach inside this scar to yesterday,
Tell me, how did that child feel,
Can you explain how a child could play.

Now look at the one whom I loved most,
Tell me, could you go on another day,
After being molested by one so close,
And later he had nothing to say.

Healing

And there will be a day,
You look to me for strength,
I give to you my courage,
You look to me for kind words,
UI give to you precious memories,
You give to me your thoughts of today,
I give to you encouragement for tomorrow,
You give me your precious love,
Oh – adults abused as children.

This day has opened the book of the past,
And today it will close,
For you know we survived,
Now the book must close forever,
And you will feel inner strength,
And that strength give you courage,
For we shed a tear and cry,
Comforting words always by your side.

What Ever Happened

What ever happened to the love we had,
For each other, Oh! So sad,
What ever happened to the respect for one another,
For now we can't be together,
What ever happened to the trust,
For we once had between us,
What ever happened to the smiles and laughs,
For now it will never again occur,
What ever happened to all the yesterdays,
For then we had pleasant things to say,
What ever happened to today,
For somewhere we lost our way,
What ever happened to the memorable days,
For now we will journey our separate ways.
What ever will happen tomorrow,
For neither of us need any more sorrow,
What ever happened, happened; and we will be forever apart,
Yet there will always be a special place for each of us–
Within our heart.

My Family

For years I have searched for a family,
For years I have longed for love and kindness,
If only I had a family to love me,
Maybe someday I will meet a loving family and find bliss.

My life was full of love and warmth at birth,
I felt what other infants felt on that special day,
If only I knew my purse on this earth,
For yesterday, I missed my childhood and youthful play.

Oh! Mom and Dad look what you did to me,
I once had a mind of a child, so open and free,
So small, sensitive and very, very fragile,
And honest and innocent at least for a while.

All I ever wanted from you was a family,
In return, I gave to you my purity and innocence,
I guess you never really wanted me,
But I did love you in my own special way.

To my family, I always offered my heart,
So very fragile and easily torn apart,
I now know what holds a family together,
That inner love shared by a family forever.

My family continues to flow with jealousy and anger's cruelty,
My family never knowing the true feeling of inner peace,
My family can live in turmoil without me,
My family, oh! My family, you can travel life's journey without me.

Tomorrow

As I journey into the past,
There isn't much left anymore,
Just the torn fragments of my mind,
Appearing and disappearing from another time.
There is a new tomorrow,
For yesterday and today have passed forever,
There will be new hope and a new rainbow,
I feel it within, I know it to be so.
I will find a new direction,
A peacefulness, which so few could ever know.
There will be someone who cares, understands, a true love,
Yes, someone who was sent to me from above,
As I occasionally journey the past,
I will continue to sadly cry,
For the hurt will never leave me,
But now I have strength to cope and I don't wish to die.
For tomorrow I will help other lonely souls of abuse,
They, too, need help with their deep sorrow,
Part of my heart will comfort them,
When the storms and violent winds blow.
Tomorrow is a new beginning,
Not only for me but everyone I pas,
Tomorrow is unborn, for me and you,
Tomorrow you may need me and I may need you.

THE GATES OF HELL

(Those innocently committed
To state mental hospitals

THE GATES OF HELL

Sweet song I sing
To myself,
Walking softly, but swiftly
Crying and crying
To myself,
Tears fall to the pavement,
And others' tears remain dry
As we approach,
THE GATES OF HELL.
The soul now weak and helpless
The mind once indestructible
So fragile_____
Now cracks,
No value, only stress.
The heart once tender,
Now broken more or less,
And swiftly approaching,
THE GATES OF HELL.
One feels a loneliness,
Within the soul,
Yes, a disbelief.
Through the door _____,
Or not,
Once so strong, now lifeless;
Crawling through the door,
Now a needle and then another,
Such distress--a lull.
One hiding behind a door,
A mongoloid is he,
Dressed in rags, dirty pants, and
A torn shirt,

Holding a couple of dolls
Lines carved deep into his face,
Still a faint smile,
Only to be lying and laughing
In the hallway,
No one to help,
Solving life's problems his
Own way.
Doctor's walk around him
Nurses walk over him,
Visitors sing a song
And dance around him,
Clergy mumble and ignore him,
No consolation, no respect
Within THE GATES OF HELL.
For me or
The crippled mongoloid.
Others with such hurt
Feel it in their face,
Human suffering and,
Disgrace
To be saved by His grace.
Assuming everything, expecting nothing,
Scuffling of feet,
Sweet sound I sing,
To mental patients I meet,
For their plight is cold
And courage so true
A faith so bold
And some, yes, you even knew.
One's soul so deep,
Yet, the staff so shallow,
One's sanity can't keep,
And everyone knows so.
For one's life in jeopardy
When all around,

My God! Nowhere to flee.
Now darkness, a lockdown,
What sadness surrounds me,
To reach for something,
In darkness I sit,
Just hearing a constant ringing,
Dear God! What is happening to me?
A flickering, then more flickering,
The faces so dismal,
And scars upon scars,
Within one, so much turmoil,
Behind a locked door
So weak and needy,
Those so drugged, so ill.
Secure environment, not free
A few insane, could kill,
Some out of touch,
With reality
Rapists, thieves, offenders,
Some seeking, others escaping,
Some naked, some dressed in furs,
A body but no being,
Confusion, disbelieve,
No respect, only
Human suffering,
No honor, no dignity
To keep.
And now----
Another cry----
Another yell ----
Another needle ----
And another----
And again, no rest,
Within these
GATES OF HELL.

ISOLATION

White walls, ceiling padded,
No sound but only one's faint voice,
Mine,
Barely alive—mentally,
Nearly dead—physically,
So quiet—no sound
But a breath—a far,
Within the walls of isolation.
The world stops for a moment,
A day, a week, a meaning none,
MY GOD! MY GOD!
A world within a world,
Deep beyond THE GATES OF HELL.
Such few could journey
No need to cry—only mourn,
And only Him to comfort me,
Quiet, loneliness, reminiscing,
Anger, forgiveness, love, now
Hatred;
For when life began.
'Cause once alive—now dead
More or less,
'Cause no value—none,
Today alive—tonight exist,
And tomorrow!
Surrounded by isolated padded
Walls,
Somewhere within,
THE GATES OF HELL.

INSTITUTIONALIZED

The world evolves—no destiny in
Sight,
Lakes, rivers, oceans, moving but
Stationary,
And as day elapses into night,
Doctors, nurses, pacing in a hurry,
For what I do not know,
'Cause the world revolves in
Circular motion,
And now through the blurred amber glass
I see,
Earth's green grass, flower and
Foliage,
Still some trees suffering
Still uplifted,
And calm,
For nature never seems to be
Agreeing,
With man and his destruction.
'Cause natural beauty lies with the
Beholder,
And man's heart has no
Conception,
Whereas his selfishness is no
Reminder,
Of God's creation when life began

But within these dark
GATES OF HELL,
I feel isolation, oppression,
Yet,
Within my sight, my reach,
Nature and its buoyant beauty so
Evident,
Of life, when it just began.

MENTAL PATIENTS

I

They don't look up—or around,
For they have no awareness,
Just loneliness, looking down,
Mental patients,
Walking around and around.
Some hug—a few kiss,
And some may clown!
Others troubled—may cry,
While most go around and around.
Some are happy—for awhile,
Still some want to die,
Yet, a few have a smile,
An evil smile,
While a few go around and around.
Some are considerate and caring,
Within a world of their own,
Having nothing but sharing,
A smile, a laugh, a cry,
Hurts upon hurts, never alone,
With THE GATES OF HELL.
And no outsider to one's rescue,
'Cause outsiders focus on the unseen,
While the world goes around and around.

II

Mental patients—a secure
Environment,
And within these dreary,
GATES OF HELL,
Some willingly, some unwillingly
Some sent,
And family nor friends
Ever utter a word,
As the world goes around and around
The progress of mental patients,
'Cause they, too, go around and around
In their own world.
And those of the outside world
Look down only to the ground
And notice their own footprints
In one's beloved own city or town.
But God protects the mental patient
While others turn away,
For God walks beside the mentally ill,
While others walk away.
Yes, He sees sunken footprints,
Of all mankind, that just go,
Around and around.

THE INSANE

Say little, trust no one
Constantly pray--,
To a Higher Power.
Today here,
Tomorrow already gone,
In the mental ward,
Deep within,
THE GATES OF HELL.
And tempers begin to flare,
Some so unkind,
Approach if you dare,
A heart filled with grief,
No home, no kin, no friend,
No help.
Deep within THE GATES OF HELL.
Some ashamed, some guilty,
Raging tempers! Confusion,
And all alone—crippled,
No strength left,
Somewhere deep within
THE GATES OF HELL.

DARKNESS

Solitude, just solitude,
Now blind and deaf,
To the lost soul,
Depressed, oppressed,
Like a beggar,
No course—just existing,
Hour after hour,
Still no direction,
A call, visit, a card, just anyone!
Someone lift this depression,
Yeah! A mental patient—and
Everyone hides,
'Cause I am deep inside the
GATES OF HELL.
Yet, the world laughs and cries,
My world, Oh! My world dies,
And oppressed by,
A dark cloud,
I remain in solitude,
Somewhere within
THE GATES OF HELL.

THE REAL WORLD

Somewhere with THE GATES OF HELL,
One can escape—all the yesterdays,
Of the real world,
Where mean-spirited people roam,
But alone and challenged,
I fought those of mean spirit,
Of the real world and
Won my freedom.
Only left feeling unsafe, insecure,
Outside—
THE GATES OF HELL.
For now frightened, all alone
'Cause no place for me,
To call my home
In the real world—where
Lost souls so sensitive,
Yet naked—,
Only mourn and mourn,
To an unsung tune,
Somewhere,
Within the real world.

IN MY DREAMS

I

Within THE GATES OF HELL and
In my dreams,
A man appeared bursting with a
Smile.
I asked his name but no response,
For he was deaf, dumb, and blind.
I thought in my dream,
How blest I am,
For I can hear, I have a mind, I can see
Why,
Should I grieve.

II

And in my dreams,
A young lady appeared,
And smiled,
She hobbled and fell to the floor,
Suffering with a muscular
Disease,
How blest I am,
For I can walk,
Why,
Should I grieve.

III

And in my dreams,
An older man appeared and smiled,
He could not speak—no mind left,
Destroyed by drugs of yesteryears
Gone-by,
How blest I am,
For I have a mind,
Why,
Should I grieve.

WHEN CLOWNS CRY

Once a child,
Always a child,
At heart.
Never foreseeing, only speculating
To be a clown—,
Someday,
Under the big top,
Looking sad, but oh! So happy,
Making others laugh,
Children,
Young and old.
But when the circus,
Arrived in town
Now an adult,
Still a child—,
At heart,
Now in the funny farm, you see,
Once a dream, now a reality;
'Cause looking on the outside,
Clowns laugh
And inside,
Clowns cry,
This day—clowns cry.

MY PAST

My past—inside the closet,
They ask—probing—staff you
Know.
Questioning when life began,
And quivering, never at ease.
Questions intense—frightened,
My words flow, mumbling—,
Jumbling—passing time,
Each of us sweating and
Sweating,
To an unsung tune—,
And looking for a
Hidden sign,
Of the unknown past.

MISTREATED

My lips mute, do not tell,
The many secrets of life's way,
The clouds have hung low,
And my body wrestled the storm,
Within THE GATES OF HELL.
For emotions have been mixed,
And mingled in turbulent streams,
Of yesterday and today,
And maybe tomorrow.
But by His grace--,
I somehow survived, I observed
And silent,
No more
To the weeps, the scars, the suffering,
And misfortunes of
Those mistreated,
Abused,
Mentally, verbally, physically,
Within the state mental hospital,
Somewhere
Inside THE GATES OF HELL.

TODAY IS MINE

Today is mine, a gift to me,
Today I choose, I will
I love, I share, I prove, I care,
My day I must fulfill.

The choice is mine, which parts I take,
How much I'll have to give,
Or do I die, or do I try,
The best I can to live.

Today is mine, I will, I will,
If God shall will that I do,
Dear God! Your love almost got away,
Oh! So divine! Please stay, don't go away.

Today is mine
And I must share,
And give and help,
And heal,
And share some more,
Yes, open my door,
And share what others
Must feel.

Yes, I must prove,
I care, I do,
And it will be a sign
That I can conquer
Anything
Because surely,
Today IS mine.

Frank Alexander Wray
1987

GO TELL

Go tell my Mother,
Her son wrongfully committed
And no tear to be shed,
For I will survive
'cause sweet sound sparrows will sing
To me, this gloomy day in spring.

Go tell my Father,
No shame leaves his name,
No sorrow, only pride,
For through my stormy life
I gave as he by my side,
And his only son will survive.

Go tell my sisters
Of my lost hour
Within these Gates of Hell;
For their smiles in misty years
Gone-by; soothes the pain
And give me cheering power.

Go tell my friends
Of boyhood years,
My battles have begun
For strong of courage,
I will not lie down
Or die.

Go tell the world
My learning, wisdom, truth,
Will someday surface
Beyond these Gates of Hell;
Then my duty will be done
And my final victory won.

THE INNOCENT

(Those innocently confined
to the state penal system)

THE INNOCENT

And the black man said,
"From every mountainside,
Let freedom ring."
Cuffs and shackles
Chains a dragging,
Sing a song
Over and over
To the tune of
Clitter and clatter
Unheard, drowned,
To the cold pavement.
Like the far-reaching pine
Singing to the open sky,
Way into the Heavens,
To the tune of Heavenly
Chimes and
Also unheard.
But the black man said,
"Let freedom ring."
There are
Days unborn, poems unwritten
Songs unsung
And souls forgiven
And unforgiven.
There are
Songs which sing,
"He Ain't Heavy, He's my Brother."
Where is my loved one,
Humming.
There are poems waiting for an Angel's tongue
Songs sweeter than ever sung,

And beautiful days hidden away
Today I sing and pray.
There are
Sweet sounds He giveth,
Comforting a suffering spirit,
A peacefulness surrounds one,
Yes, the innocent liveth.
Perhaps life is like a river
Deep and wide.
Our loved ones on every tide
They said from my sight,
Singing, singing, "far away."
Yet gentle airs, so sweet, so calm, and
I mourn and feel a breath of balm, and
Soothed sorrow dries a tear,
For I hear tunes, blended notes
Somewhere beyond this river—
A soft tune—a transparent melody.
Speak softly;
Let the words sing,
Just whisper, not a yell,
Endure, turn the other cheek,
And never, ever tell,
Always remember,
Let freedom ring.
In time of storms of hope and fear,
We need a smile to shed a tear,
And one's wounded pride
Remains still,
Don't you see, its His will.
And as day merges to night,
And an Angel guides me by
Light,
Reminding, He does all things well,
For the black man was right,

The end shall soon tell.
If only one could see;
The deep scars over my brow
Or feel the hurt I endure now,
Or how I sadly cry now,
But I recall what the black man said:
"Let freedom ring."
If only one could see,
How the sun has shown through
The shadow,
The true beauty of a rainbow
The hills I climbed in days of rain,
And how He has been by my side.
If only one knew,
The tears and tears and
The silent fears,
How those I once loved
Were so wrong, but
I survived, I am innocent.
My child's picture, my child
A gift to me,
Her precious lips—soft face,
Her little hands and tender touch
Now walking, graciously, laughing,
My God, I love her so much.
But the black man says--,
"Let freedom ring."
Oh! inmate, Oh! friend of mine,
Dry your tears, calm your grief,
Place your cares on Him alone
For He will give you strength,
And guard and guide you to the end.
Oh! inmate, Oh! friend of mine,
Your battle not lost, so weep,
Let tears of sorrow fall,

For a black man once said,
"Let freedom ring."
Your innocence will set you free,
And ring to the four corners,
You are free!
The black man was right—
Time will set you free.
Journey have I—
A dark and humble beginning
For torn between two worlds,
One I wish to leave and
One hesitant to enter.
The doorway the same
Now lost—
Between the two,
For neither world--,
Sets me free, but
Each pulling gently,
To set me free.
Time.
No longer on my side
Yet, a constant reminder
Of accomplishments,
Failures,
Running away, to the unseen,
Reaching toward an unborn day,
Whistling to the tune,
The sweet song of
A precision Swiss clock,
Ticking slowly, softly, gently,
Within the penal system 'cause
Time—will end soon,
As waiting becomes eternally quenched
And time approaches—
Heavenly Eternity.

Heaviness, heaviness, such heaviness, absorbs me,
Not knowing—only speculating--,
To be free someday,
Waiting, silence, a distant bit of laughter,
Briefly,
No mail again today, just reminiscing
Of years gone by, forever
Waiting for something, knowing nothing,
Those,
No compassion for humanity and
Within the realms of prison wall,
A glass dome
Hangs over my world,
As wind-torn clouds
Hang low, to a lost soul,
And as night again turns to day
A year turns into another decade
And I remain innocent;
Yet, the black man says;
"Let freedom ring
On every hillside."
Let the song sing,
Free, yes, free;
I am free, at last,
Dear God, I have earned my
VICTORY!

THE END

"FROM WISDOM COMES STRENGTH."
–Frank A. Wray.

EPILOGUE

There is nothing imaginary written within the pages of this factual book of verse. This book was written with the sole intention of reaching out to the many people held in captivity and against their will. The book shows the reader the turmoil and life-going effects of human suffering. With this in mind, the reader will gain a profound knowledge of the despairing subject, and the reader will then have to imagine being in the same situation of the victim, if possible. At that moment, the reader will realize the statement from Einstein: "Imagination is greater than knowledge."

I wrote this book from my observations of those placed in confinement and left with a heavy heart. Hopefully, these words will someday show the reader that a wrong direction taken in a dreadful storm can be overcome with love, trust, and kindness all within a safe environment.

Within the realm of evolution, it is true: good and evil do not mix and within the two worlds, only one will prevail. The victim is given the knowledge of his or her surroundings, but the creativity of imagination is far greater than knowledge for survival during a tragedy.

Today, I continue to explore all the avenues of my love, the craft of writing. It is with much pleasure I can walk freely along Saint Augustine, Florida and gain a sense of insight to write a book.